CHRISTMAS CRACKERS.

THE BRAN PIE

DRESSED FOR A CHARADE.

UNDER THE MISTLETOE.

SLIDING

FAIRY GIFTS FROM SANTA CLAUS.

WILLIAM COLLINS SONS & CO LTD
London Glasgow Sydney Auckland
Toronto Johannesburg

First published 1979
© Elizabeth Walter, 1979
ISBN 0 00 216 196 6

Designed by Trevor Vincent
Made and printed in Great Britain by
W. S. Cowell Ltd, Ipswich

The illustrations of Victorian and Edwardian
Christmas cards and scraps are reproduced
by courtesy of the Mansell Collection,
Ronald Clark and John Vincent.

A Christmas Scrapbook

Compiled by ELIZABETH WALTER

COLLINS

St James's Place, London

1979

Christmas Day

CHRISTMAS (Christ's Mass) was not celebrated in the early church. Not until the year 354 was the Nativity officially celebrated in Rome on December 25, but the true date and even the year of Christ's birth are unknown. It undoubtedly occurred some 4-14 years earlier than the year One. Christ was born 'in the days when Herod was king of Judaea' – and Herod died in 4 BC. He was also born at a time when 'there went out a decree from Caesar Augustus that all the world should be taxed.' Historians date this census at some point in the years 7-11 BC. Christmas is older than we think it is.

Saturnalia

A HAPPY CHRISTMAS.

THE Ancient Roman feast of the god Saturn was held on December 17. For several days thereafter schools and law courts were closed, war was outlawed, there was much eating and drinking, and slaves and their masters ate at the same table, the masters often waiting on the slaves. Gifts from master to servant were also a feature of the festivities. A more general exchange of gifts among equals took place at the Kalends of January, our New Year.

When the Christian cult of the Nativity developed, many of the elements of the Roman Saturnalia proved entirely compatible, and because of the nearness of the date were absorbed into it.

Yule

ULE comes from an Old Norse word *jól*. This was a winter feast lasting twelve days, held at the time of the Winter Solstice (December 21) when the sun is at its greatest distance from the equator and – especially in Northern latitudes – appears to stand still. The rekindling of fire on the hearth or altar was an important element of this feast, and has survived in the form of the Yule log, which in the days of wide fireplaces and big chimneys was often borne in ceremoniously wreathed with evergreen.

A little of the log was burnt on each of the twelve days of Christmas. But:

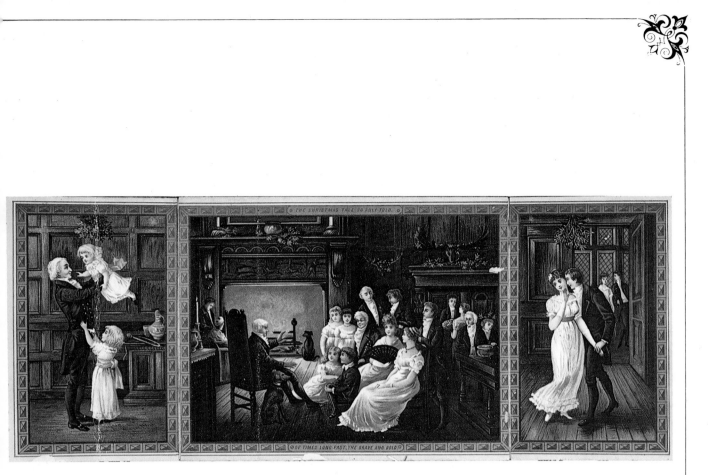

Part must be kept wherewith to tend
The Christmas Log next year;
And where 'tis safely kept, the Fiend
Can do no mischief there.

from THE CEREMONIES FOR CANDLEMAS DAY by Robert Herrick

Those who find the twelve days of Christmas too much might care to reflect that as late
as the seventeenth century the 'Christmas season' lasted till February 2 – Candlemas Day.

Nowell

Nowell, nowell, nowell, nowell,
This is the salutation of
The Angel Gabriel.

OLD CAROL

THE old name for Christmas, also used as an exclamation of joy at that season, comes from the Latin *dies natalis*, natal day. In the more modern form Noël it is the French name for Christmas, and Father Christmas is *le père Noël*.

PEACE! HOLY ANGELS HOVER NEAR

Old Christmas

IN September 1752 England, in common with most of Western Europe, changed from the Julian to the Gregorian calendar, which meant that twelve days were 'lost' and everything became correspondingly earlier. What had always been December 25 was now January 6, so that Epiphany occurred on what had previously been Christmas Day. The change was much resented by country people, and for well over a hundred years Old Christmas (January 6) was the real day of celebration in rural areas.

Nature also resented the change. The animals were said to kneel and the Glastonbury Thorn to blossom on Old Christmas Eve, regardless of what men did with the calendar.

To add to the complications, Russia and most of Eastern Europe did not adopt the Gregorian calendar until February 1918.

A merry Christmas.

Dissenting Voices

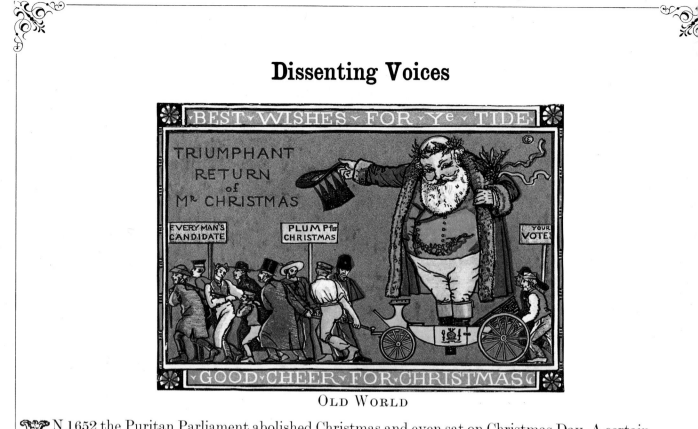

OLD WORLD

IN 1652 the Puritan Parliament abolished Christmas and even sat on Christmas Day. A certain Hezekiah Woodward, in a tract of 1656, calls Christmas Day 'The old Heathens' Feasting Day, in honour of Saturn, their Idol-God, the Papists' Massing Day, the Profane Man's Ranting Day, the Superstitious Man's Idol Day, the Multitude's Idle Day, Satan's – that Adversary's – Working Day, the True Christian Man's Fasting Day . . .' The worthy Hezekiah concludes: 'We are persuaded, no one thing more hindereth the Gospel work all the year long, than doth the observation of that Idol Day once in a year, having so many days of cursed observation with it.'

NEW WORLD

In 1659 in Puritan Massachusetts the General Court fined people for observing Christmas and decreed: 'Anybody who is found observing, by abstinence from labour, feasting, or in any other way, any such days as Christmas Day, shall pay for every such offence five shillings.'

Nevertheless, when it came to the vote, Christmas won hands down on both sides of the Atlantic.

Reindeer

SANTA CLAUS'S steeds are natives of the Arctic, but it is to the United States that we owe the concept of the reindeer-drawn sleigh, popularized though not necessarily originated by Clement Clarke Moore's poem *A Visit from St Nicholas*, first published in 1823. This lists the eight reindeer's names as Dasher, Dancer, Prancer, Vixen, Comet, Cupid, Donder and Blitzen.

Rudolph the Red-Nosed Reindeer is a late addition to the team. He did not make his appearance until 1939, when the song of that name was first published.

Reindeer are the only deer in which both sexes have antlers. They stand about four feet high at the shoulder and are immensely strong, well able to pull twice their own weight on a sled. In winter their hoofs become concave, making them sure-footed even on ice. Does this also explain their well-known ability to scale snow-clad roofs?

Santa Claus

All you wish, I wish for you.
Many glad surprises too;
Peace, and Plenty, Mirth,
, and Play

Be your
portion
every-
day!

E. Blomfield.

He comes in the night! He comes in the night!
　　He softly, silently comes;
While the little brown heads on the pillows so white
　　Are dreaming of bugles and drums . . .
And yet not the sound of a drum is heard,
　　Not a bugle blast is blown,
As he mounts to the chimney-top like a bird,
　　And drops to the hearth like a stone.

ANON

SANTA CLAUS is an American. The gift-bringer's name is a corruption of St Nicholas, the pronunciation of the name by nineteenth-century Dutch settlers having been misunderstood.

Nicholas was a fourth-century bishop of Myra in Asia Minor, who devoted the large fortune left him by wealthy parents to helping the poor. But he preferred to do good by stealth. One day, hearing that a poor man was reduced to selling his three pretty daughters as slaves, Nicholas threw three purses of gold through the door. On another occasion, on a midnight do-gooding expedition, he threw some gold coins down a chimney and they fell into a stocking (some say a shoe) which had been put in the hearth to dry. This is the origin of our Christmas stockings.

After the good bishop's death, the secret of his benefactions leaked out and it became the custom to give presents in secret on his feast day, December 6, and make believe St Nicholas was the donor. In many Continental countries the present-giving still takes place on December 6 and has a ritual of its own, but in England and America it has become part of the Christmas celebrations.

The three purses of gold are commemorated also in the three gold balls of pawnbrokers' trade signs, for St Nicholas is their patron saint – as he is of children, especially orphans, of merchants, bakers, sailors, parish clerks, of Russia before the Revolution, and of the city of Amsterdam.

We owe Santa Claus's traditional appearance to another American, Thomas Nast, whose drawing of him, complete with white beard, fur-trimmed robe and toys, appeared in *Harper's Magazine* in the 1860's and became the prototype.

Santa Claus is also the name of a town in Indiana, USA, founded by German settlers in 1852 and named on Christmas Eve. In 1935 a giant Santa Claus statue was erected in the town park, dedicated to 'the children of the world in memory of an undying love'. The town runs a week's training course for prospective Santas, and those who pass the exam receive a diploma – 'Bachelor of Santa Claus' – and are much in demand in stores and at parties.

Carols

WISHING YOU A HAPPY CHRISTMAS

THE word carol comes from the Latin *caraula* and meant originally a singing dance characterized by a vigorous rhythm and a regularly repeated refrain – for example, *The First Nowell* and *I Saw Three Ships*. Carols were always joyful and not necessarily of religious significance – there were carols for May Day and Midsummer too.

The Reformation and later Puritanism dealt a serious blow to this folk music, but carols lived on in oral tradition, often debased, until the revival of interest in folk music in the last century led to their being rescued and added to the body of Christmas hymns such as *Christians, Awake* and *Hark, the Herald Angels Sing* which had developed independently. Today the distinction between hymn and carol has disappeared.

We owe the Festival of Nine Lessons and Carols to Edward White Benson, first Bishop of Truro, who devised a service of readings and carols in the 1880's to create a sense of tradition in his newly formed diocese. When he became Archbishop of Canterbury, the idea spread to the college chapels of his old university, Cambridge. Broadcasting has made the candlelit Christmas Eve service from King's College Chapel known all over the world.

'Silent Night'

Wishing you a Happy CHRISTMAS.

HIS beloved carol was first performed in the village church of Oberndorf, near Salzburg, on Christmas Eve, 1818. It was scored originally for two voices and a guitar.

The words were written by Father Joseph Mohr, the 28-year-old parish priest, and they were set to music by Franz Xaver Gruber, the schoolmaster from the neighbouring village of Arnsdorf, who was also the organist.

The guitar accompaniment is due to the church mice who had been at the organ and put it temporarily out of action!

Waits

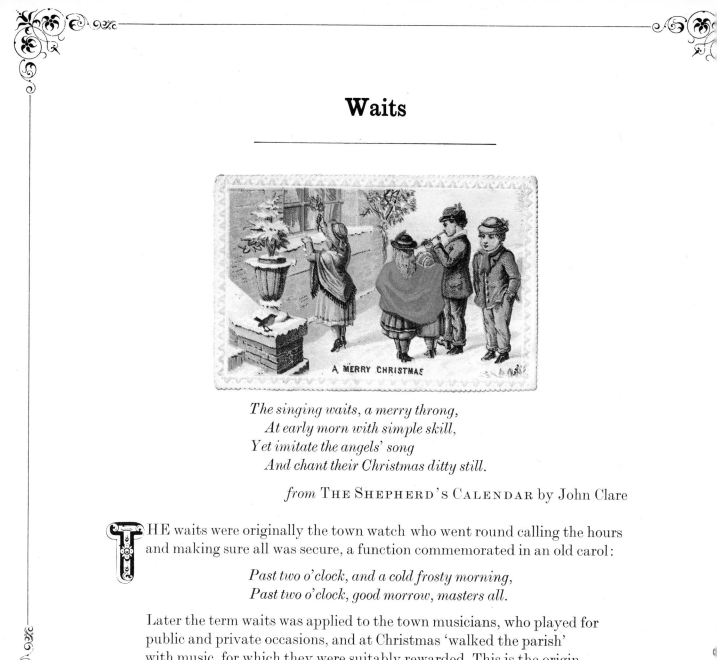

A MERRY CHRISTMAS

The singing waits, a merry throng,
At early morn with simple skill,
Yet imitate the angels' song
And chant their Christmas ditty still.

from THE SHEPHERD'S CALENDAR by John Clare

THE waits were originally the town watch who went round calling the hours and making sure all was secure, a function commemorated in an old carol:

Past two o'clock, and a cold frosty morning,
Past two o'clock, good morrow, masters all.

Later the term waits was applied to the town musicians, who played for public and private occasions, and at Christmas 'walked the parish' with music, for which they were suitably rewarded. This is the origin of carol-singing parties, whether by adults collecting for charity, or by children collecting for themselves.

The Christmas Crib

ST FRANCIS of Assisi erected the first Christmas Crib in a cave on a hillside outside the town of Grecchio on December 24, 1224. This charming custom has since spread all over the world.

'What shall we bring thee, O Christ, when Thou art born on
earth as man for our sake; for each of the creatures who have
their being from Thee gives thanks to Thee: angels their songs,
the heavens a star, the Wise Men gifts, the shepherds wonder,
the earth a cave, the wilderness a manger, but we – the Virgin Mother.'

from the CHRISTMAS VESPERS *of the Greek Orthodox Church*

The Holly and The Ivy

The holly and the ivy,
When they are both well grown,
Of all the trees that are
in the wood
The holly bears the crown.

OLD CAROL

BOTH the Romans and the Norsemen decorated their houses and temples with evergreen on festive occasions, evergreen symbolizing perpetual life, especially in the dead days of winter. But few people who sing *The Holly and the Ivy*

realize that this is a Christian take-over of a carol commemorating an age-old pagan battle between male and female principles in the vegetable kingdom, symbolized by the holly (male) and the ivy (female). The holly won, of course! Traces of this contest also survive in a fifteenth-century poem:

Nay, ivy, nay,
It shall not be, iwis,
Holly hath the mastery
As the manner is.

Or, as the carol has it:

Of all the trees that are
in the wood
The holly bears the crown.

Mistletoe

The mistletoe hung in the castle hall,
The holly branch shone on the old oak wall.

from THE MISTLETOE BOUGH *by Thomas Haynes Bayly*

THIS parasitic plant, *Viscum album*, its berries beloved by the birds, has magical associations going as far back as the Druids. It usually grows on apple trees, occasionally on ash trees, but the plant prized by the Druids had to grow on an oak, which is extremely rare. Its magical properties were only preserved if it was cut with a golden knife.

Because of its pagan associations, mistletoe has never been used in church decorations.

CHRISTMAS PEACE AND CHRISTMAS PLEASURE BE WITH YOU IN BOUNDLESS MEASURE.

Our practice of kissing under the mistletoe is an obvious survival of an old fertility rite.

The Christmas Tree

THE Christmas tree comes from Germany. St Boniface in the eighth century is said to have substituted a young fir-tree as a symbol of the new Christian faith for a sacred pagan oak which he cut down one Christmas Eve.

Martin Luther in the early sixteenth century fostered the cult by using a candlelit tree as an image of the starlit heaven from which Christ came, thus ensuring the Christmas tree's continued popularity in Protestant areas.

Hessian contingents in the English army took the idea to America during the War of Independence, well before it reached England, which it did via German merchants and Court officials in the 1820's.

It was the Prince Consort, however, who made the tree a part of English Christmas celebrations almost overnight, when he married Queen Victoria in 1840 and introduced a tree as part of the Royal Family's Christmas.

Christmas Flowers

HEALTH and Happiness this CHRISTMAS Day.

THE CHRISTMAS ROSE, *Helleborus niger*, is of alpine origin and blooms from December to March, even in snow. The flowers vary from pure white to pink. Its regular appearance despite adverse weather was so impressive that the whole plant was considered sacred, and it was believed to be effective against both plague and evil spirits. Its black root (which gives the plant its name of black hellebore), when dried and powdered, causes violent sneezing.

In recent years the Christmas cult of the poinsettia has spread from North America. This scarlet-flowered plant comes from Mexico, where Dr Poinsett discovered it in 1828. Its Mexican name was Flower of the Holy Night.

Christmas Cards

THE first Christmas card, intended to be sent via the penny post which had been instituted in 1840, was produced by Henry Cole, founder of the Victoria and Albert Museum, in 1843. The hand-coloured lithograph was designed by John Calcott Horsley, R.A., and sold at Felix Summerley's Treasure House in Bond Street, in which Cole had a financial interest, price one shilling. It was a commercial failure.

But the idea of Christmas cards did not die, and by 1860 they had become established, as the new printing process of chromolithography enabled the cards, often printed on the Continent, to be both elaborate and cheap. In 1870 the halfpenny post was introduced for cards sent in unsealed envelopes, and the Christmas card really came into its own. By 1880 the Postmaster General was having to issue the first 'Post Early for Christmas' plea.

The fashion for mounting Christmas cards in albums, which developed from the 1860's on, changed the design of cards. Early cards were not much more than decorated visiting cards and sold at one penny each, but now the picture became all-important and verses and greetings were transferred to the back.

In recent years the issue of Christmas cards by various charities has contributed substantially to their revenue.

Robins

THE ubiquitous bird on Christmas stationery has no direct connection with Christmas, except that, since robins choose their mates as early as December, their plumage and song are at their best in a season when other birds' are dull and mute. Because of its red breast, the robin was reputed in Western Europe to be one of the birds that brought fire to earth, and hence lucky, especially at the time of the winter solstice.

The introduction of the penny post in 1840 also led to the robin being used as a symbol on Christmas cards. Early postmen wore royal red uniforms and were sometimes called 'Robin Postman'.

Turkey

THE turkey does not come from Turkey. It gets its name from its cry of 'turk-turk' and is a native of Mexico. The conquistadors found it already domesticated there and were quick to appreciate its excellence and bring it back to Europe.

It reached England in the early sixteenth century. Henry VIII is the first person recorded to have dined on turkey on Christmas Day.

The bird seems to have found favour with royalty. Some two hundred years later George II kept a large flock of turkeys in Richmond Park – for shooting!

Goose

'There's *such* a goose, Martha!'
from A CHRISTMAS CAROL by Charles Dickens

HURRAH! FOR A MERRY CHRISTMAS!

LTHOUGH now superseded by turkey, goose was the traditional English Christmas bird for almost three hundred years. It became associated with celebration because Queen Elizabeth I was feasting on goose at Greenwich Palace on Christmas Eve, 1588, when news was brought to her of the final destruction of the Spanish Armada. She decreed that from then on roast goose should be served at Christmas.

The custom spread from England to Germany, where goose is still the favourite fare.

Christmas Pudding

May your Christmas Party be jolly and happy.

A smell like an eating-house and a pastrycook's next door
to each other, with a laundress's next door to that.
That was the pudding.

from A CHRISTMAS CAROL by Charles Dickens

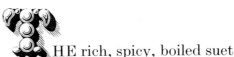

THE rich, spicy, boiled suet pudding is one of the oldest English traditions, though its present form goes back only to the seventeenth century. George I, who was offered the Crown in December 1714, was known as the Pudding King, and the pudding served to him at his first English Christmas contained the following ingredients:

$1\frac{1}{2}$ lbs shredded suet, 1 lb of eggs weighed in their shells, 1 lb each of dried plums stoned and halved, mixed peel cut in strips, small raisins, sultanas, currants, flour, sugar and brown breadcrumbs, 1 teaspoonful of mixed spice, 1 nutmeg grated, 2 teaspoonfuls of salt, 1 pint of new milk, juice of 1 lemon, and a very large wineglassful of brandy.

Puddings made at home are stirred by every member of the family and each makes a wish. Traditionally, they were made on the last Sunday of Advent, which was known as Stir-Up Sunday from the Collect for the day beginning 'Stir up, we beseech Thee, O Lord . . .'

> *Stir up, we beseech thee,*
> *The pudding in the pot,*
> *And when we get home*
> *We'll eat the lot.*

The risky practice of inserting silver charms or old-fashioned silver threepenny bits in puddings has fortunately died out, but there is no diminution in the popularity of dowsing the pudding with spirit and setting light to it so that it is borne blazing to the table.

Puddings have changed shape in the last hundred years. They used to be boiled in a cloth and be round as cannon-balls. Today they are basin-shaped.

Christmas Pie

Little Jack Horner
Sat in a corner,
Eating his Christmas pie.

OLD NURSERY RHYME

C HRISTMAS PIE appears to have been a forerunner of mince pie in that it contained a mixture of meat, fruit and spices. A French visitor, Henri Misson, described it in 1699 as 'a most learned Mixture of Neats'-tongues, Chicken, Eggs, Sugar, Raisins, Lemon and Orange Peel, and various kinds of spicery', and says it was 'eaten everywhere'.

So when Little Jack Horner 'put in his thumb and pulled out a plum', he seems to have had the right dish – though the 'plum' he extracted was a rich manor. The Abbot of Glastonbury, seeking to placate the predatory Henry VIII, sent him the deeds of several manors in a Christmas pie. Horner, his steward, was charged with delivering it . . .

The nursery rhyme was originally a satirical comment on the affair.

Mincé Pie

Drink now the strong Beer,
Cut the white loaf here,
The while the meat is a-shredding;
For the rare Mince Pie
And the Plums stand by
To fill the Paste that's a-kneading.

from CEREMONIES FOR CHRISTMAS
by Robert Herrick

MINCEMEAT no longer contains meat, as in Herrick's day, but is a survivor of the mediaeval taste for mixing meat with fruit and spices, often for preservative reasons, as well as reasons of flavour.

He who eats twelve mince pies in twelve different houses during the twelve days of Christmas will have twelve happy months in the coming year.

Crackers

A LATE addition to the Christmas festivities. They originated in France, when a bag of bon-bons was enclosed in a paper wrapper which two children could pull apart (A cracker is still a bon-bon in France). In the 1860's an English firm had the idea of adding a snap, or cracker, to create a tiny explosion when the paper wrapper gave way.

Wishing you a very happy Christmas.

Wassail

The wassail round, in good brown bowls,
Garnished with ribbons, blithely trowls.

from MARMION *by Sir Walter Scott*

THE word wassail comes from two Anglo-Saxon words, *was hael* –
be thou hale; hence Good Health! a salutation offered with a drink,
particularly one presented in a bowl which was passed from hand to
hand as everyone drank in fellowship.

The traditional content of the bowl was lambswool, a concoction
of hot ale, spices, sugar, eggs and roasted apples, to which cream and
sippets of toast were sometimes added. The custom became
associated with Christmas ('when roasted crabs hiss in the bowl' –
Shakespeare), and so did the word wassail.

Children collecting pennies at that season would go a-wassailing,
wishing good health to those they called on hopefully.

Love and joy come to you,
And to you your wassail too,
And God bless you and send you
A Happy New Year.

OLD CAROL

Southern Comfort

GG NOG is a Christmas institution in the American South, which welcomed Christmas more readily than the Puritan North. Alabama was the first State to make December 25 a legal holiday – in 1863. Oklahoma was the last – in 1890.

Egg Nog is traditionally prepared and dispensed by the man of the house. Here is a recipe from Florida:

Separate 6 medium-sized eggs.

Whip whites till stiff and set aside.

Beat yolks, adding 6 tablespoonfuls of caster sugar and 12 tablespoonfuls of bourbon whisky (or brandy).

Whip one pint of double cream until moderately thick.

Fold in egg mixture, then whites, and dust with nutmeg.

Christmas Geography

I wish you a joyous and happy Christmas

CHRISTMAS ISLAND is the largest coral atoll in the Pacific and one of the British Line Islands. It lies near the equator and approximately 1250 miles south of Hawaii. It was named by Captain James Cook when, on his third and last voyage of exploration, he first sighted the island on December 24, 1777. He and his crew spent Christmas there, naming the island in commemoration.

There is another, smaller Christmas Island in the Indian Ocean some 200 miles south of Java. This was first discovered by English explorers at Christmas 1643. Today it is an Australian possession. Its phosphate deposits give it a certain economic importance, whereas its larger namesake was devastated by atom bomb trials in the 1950's.

The South African province of Natal was so named by Portuguese navigators in the sixteenth century because they first sighted it on Christmas Day. *Natal* is the Portuguese word for Nativity.

The city of Natal in Brazil was named by the Portuguese for a similar reason.

They founded it on Christmas Day, 1599.

'A Christmas Carol'

THE best-known and best-beloved of all Dickens's works, *A Christmas Carol* was written in 1843 in the space of four weeks and published by Chapman and Hall with four coloured illustrations by John Leech.

It was almost immediately pirated, and appeared in a twopenny weekly, *Parley's Illuminated Library*, as 'A Christmas Ghost Story re-originated from the original by Charles Dickens, Esq., and analytically condensed expressly for this work'. Dickens sued. The publishers of the weekly claimed that they had made great improvements and additions to the original. For example, Tiny Tim had been given a song of sixty lines to sing. The original work had been 'unhinged and put together again', and 'incongruities have been tastefully remedied'.

Dickens won his case, but the defendants pleaded bankruptcy, which meant that Dickens got no damages and had to pay his own costs of £700. 'My feeling is that it is better to suffer a great wrong than to have recourse to the much greater wrong of the Law,' he wrote afterwards.

Boxing Day

A Happy Christmas

A kindly word and a cheery rhyme
To wish you a happy Christmas time.

SEVERAL explanations are offered why December 26, the feast of the first Christian martyr, St Stephen, is known as Boxing Day in England. One theory is that it was the day when the church-wardens opened the poor box, after the presumed lavishness of Christmas, and distributed its contents to the poor of the parish. Others say it was the day when servants received an additional payment – a Christmas box.

The name Boxing Day was first used in 1849. It has nothing to do with the sport of boxing.

Pantomime

There were two subordinate actors, who played,
subordinately well, the fore and hind legs of a donkey.

from THE COVENT GARDEN PANTOMIME by John Ruskin

SINCE Victorian days Pantomime traditionally opens on Boxing Day. Even before the early eighteenth century, when the first recorded one opened at Drury Lane, there was a long history of drama and spectacle associated with Christmas, from mediaeval miracle plays to the court masques of James I.

The first pantomimes were based on the figures of Harlequin, Columbine and Pantaloon, had elaborate scenery and included music, dancing, broad comedy, and a transformation scene – the same elements we know today, though the Commedia dell' Arte figures have given place to fairytale

A·Pleasant·Christmas·to·you.

S. Hildesheimer & Cᵒ   Nᵒ 231 Copyright

characters such as Aladdin, Cinderella, Ali Baba, and the Babes in the Wood.

The convention of a girl playing the hero's part – the Principal Boy – dates back to the 1820's.

In 1889 at Drury Lane a music hall actor, Dan Leno, was engaged to reverse the position and play a man burlesquing a woman: the Dame. For the rest of his life he played the Dame in every Drury Lane pantomime, and the Dame succeeded Pantaloon, the clown, as the principal comic character. Today the clown has retreated to the circus – another Christmas entertainment, though less specifically so.

A mirthful, merry time this Christmas.

S. Hildesheimer & Cº.   Nº 67. Copyright.

Bells

Ding, dong, merrily on high
In heaven the bells are ringing.

OLD CAROL

IN an age of few clocks and no media, church bells played an important part in daily life. They tolled for the dead and pealed for a wedding, proclaimed the curfew and sounded the tocsin of alarm. But at Christmas and New Year they played an especially prominent role, for they pealed merrily on Christmas morning – and still do – to proclaim the Saviour's birth, and they ring out the Old Year and ring in the New. 'Of all sounds of all bells – (bells, the music nighest bordering upon heaven) – most solemn and touching is the peal which rings out the Old Year,' claimed Charles Lamb in his essay on *New Year's Eve.*

A HAPPY CHRISTMAS

Bells are so closely associated with this season that they are a recognized Christmas symbol on cards and decorations.

More recently, the song *Jingle, Bells* has become linked with Christmas, though J. Pierpont, the nineteenth-century American author and composer, wrote it as a song of revelry and the chorus was originally accompanied by the jingling of glasses.

New Year

HEALTH AND HAPPINESS TO YOU.

NEW YEAR'S EVE – Hogmanay in Scotland – is characterized by a rousing welcome to the New Year from pealing bells, factory hooters, ships' sirens, car horns, cheering, and the singing of *Auld Lang Syne*. The noise serves to scare away the evil spirits who might otherwise slip in through the crack between the Old Year and the New.

After this the First-Footer goes round to bring luck to the houses he visits for the coming year. He – a woman is considered very unlucky – must be dark-haired. He enters by the front door, leaves by the back door, if there is one, and brings with him a lump of coal, a piece of bread, and a little money or salt, to assure the household of warmth, food and wealth.

Many early Christmas cards were, properly speaking, New Year cards, and children sometimes received their presents on that day rather than at Christmas because the Nativity was considered a purely religious occasion and such frivolities were out of place.

The Watch Night services held in some churches on New Year's Eve are not a survival from the Middle Ages. They were instituted by the Methodist Society in the eighteenth century and have been taken up by other churches since.

The Three Wise Men

THE THREE KINGS from the East may have been Wise Men, but they were not kings in our sense. They were rulers of cities or provinces – some authorities list these as Nubia and Arabia, Godolic and Sheba, and Tarse and Egypt. Nor were they necessarily three – the Bible makes no mention of number, only of their gifts. Nevertheless, most other authorities settle for the mystic three and confidently cite their names and attributes: Melchior, old and grey-bearded, who brought the gold of kingship; Caspar, young and beardless, offering frankincense for godhead; and Balthazar, the dark king who brought the myrrh of humanity and woe.

In Spain it is the Three Kings who bring the children's gifts on January 6.

Cologne Cathedral possesses the relics of the Three Kings, given by the Emperor Frederick Barbarossa in 1164, and their cult is popular throughout the Rhineland and Southern Germany. They are the special protectors of all who go on journeys.

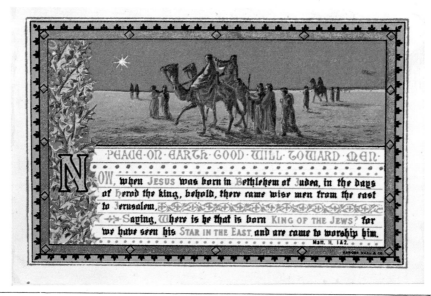

The Star of Bethlehem

May the star of Bethlehem guide thee at Christmas.

AS there really a star in the East that led the Three Wise Men to Bethlehem? Modern wise men still don't know. The star might have been Halley's Comet which is visible every 76 years and would have been especially brilliant in the East – but some twelve years before we officially date Christ's birth.

Another theory is that Saturn and Jupiter were visible in conjunction in the Sign of Pisces – but this astronomical event occurs only every 257 years, and the nearest instance would have been seven years before the birth of Christ.

So what star did the Wise Men follow?

Twelfth Night

WELFTH NIGHT is literally the night of January 5-6, the eve of the Epiphany, but for centuries it has been taken to mean January 6, the day when the Christmas decorations are taken down and Christmas comes to an end.

Today there are few ceremonies to mark it, but until the middle of the last century the highpoint of the occasion was the Twelfth Night cake, an elaborately iced confection which has now been incorporated into the Christmas cake.

On January 6, 1663, Samuel Pepys commented irritably that he 'saw *Twelfth Night* acted well, though it be but a silly play, and not relating at all to the name or day.' He had evidently forgotten Shakespeare's alternative title: *Twelfth Night, or What You Will.*

Epiphany

THE word epiphany comes from the Greek and means a showing, a manifestation. It is the thirteenth day of Christmas, the day when Christ was shown to the world represented by the Three Kings. In commemoration, gold, frankincense and

Bring the green & graceful toy,
Bring the Holly berries gay,
We must have a noble garland
For our Christmas Holiday.

myrrh are still offered on the Queen's behalf at Holy Communion in the Chapel Royal of St James's Palace.

In the Orthodox Church the Epiphany is a more important feast than the Nativity, and celebrates the Baptism of Christ.